I0794930

Eve Is Like Me

by Jesse Peebles
illustrated by Saura Ganesh

Practice Decodable 18

McGraw Hill Education

Bothell, WA • Chicago, IL • Columbus, OH • New York, NY

MHEonline.com

Send all inquiries to:
McGraw-Hill Education
8787 Orion Place
Columbus, OH 43240

ISBN: 978-0-02-144734-3
MHID: 0-02-144734-9

Printed in the United States of America.

8 9 10 CTM 23

Hope felt sad.

She did not like to be sad.

Can she find pals?

Hope met Eve.

"I am six," said Hope.

"Same as me!" said Eve.

Hope and Eve can be pals.

Eve and Hope felt glad to be pals.